green leaf

brown bear

purple
pencils

orange
carrot

The **First Skills** series includes seven books designed to help parents amuse, interest and at the same time teach their children. **Colours and shapes** and **abc** contribute to the child's early understanding of the reading process. **Counting** teaches her to recognize and understand simple numbers. **Telling the time** helps her to relate the time on a clock face to her everyday life and activities. **Big and little** deals with words that describe relative sizes and positions, all shown through objects and scenes that will be familiar to the young child. **Everyday words** helps her to enjoy and practise her vocabulary. **Verbs** will develop her early reading and language skills. In each book, bright, detailed, interesting illustrations combine with a simple and straightforward text to present fundamental concepts clearly and comprehensibly.

Talk about the colours and shapes of familiar things: 'let's put on your red socks! Which top would you like to wear today – the green one or the blue stripy one?' Talk about the shapes you see when you're playing indoors or out and about: 'look at the clock – it's round, isn't it? How many other round things can you see?'

Published by Ladybird Books Ltd
A Penguin Company
Penguin Books Ltd, 80 Strand, London WC2R 0RL, UK
Penguin Books Australia Ltd, Camberwell, Victoria, Australia
Penguin Books (NZ) Ltd, Cnr Airborne and Rosedale Roads, Albany, Auckland,
1310, New Zealand

2 4 6 8 10 9 7 5 3 1
© LADYBIRD BOOKS LTD MMVI

Printed in Italy

rectangle

This tile is rectangle shaped.

Can you see how it is different from a square?

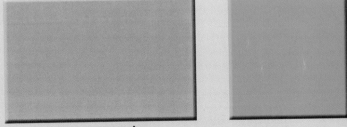

rectangle   square

Talk to your child about the differences between a rectangle (two sides long and two sides short) and a square (all sides are the same length).

Let's go on a square hunt!

painting

window

puzzle

game board

Can you find these rectangles in your house?

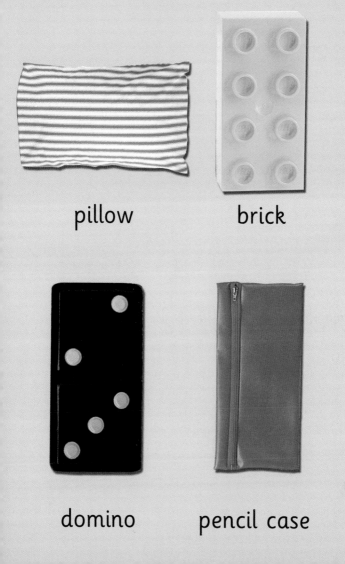

pillow

brick

domino

pencil case

A feast of colours and shapes,
what a treat!
Say the names of the shapes
you would eat.

How many triangles can you see here?

cheese

sails

pizza

party hat

square

These blocks are square shaped.

What colour squares can you see?

triangle

These tiles are triangle shaped.
They each have three corners.

Can you point to all three corners?

Trace round each circle shape with your finger.

button

cake

wheel

ball

circle

Everything around us has a shape.
This is a circle.

What colour is the circle?

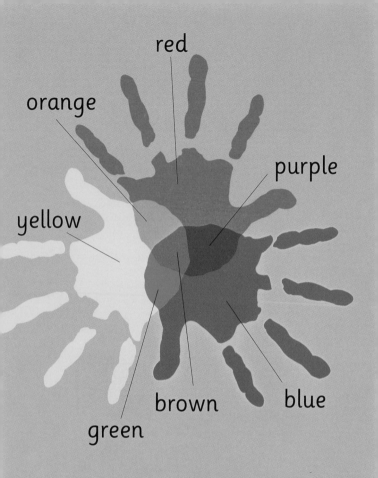

red

orange

purple

yellow

brown

green

blue

Red, blue and yellow make brown.

Help your child to create new colours by mixing paints.

Let's go on a shape hunt!
What shapes can you see here?

wheel

puzzle

pizza

domino

colours and shapes

by Lesley Clark
photography by Garie Hind
illustrations by Terry Burton

Everything has a colour. There are colours of things to play with...

colours of things to eat...

colours of things in your home...

and colours of things
in the street.

How many different colours
can you see?

red

Boots, coat, ribbons, hat –
I am dressed all in red!

Let's hunt for some more red!

red apple

red bus

red mug

red play dough

yellow

Yellow is bright, bold and fun.
Yellow is the colour of my sun.

Here are lots of yellow things.

yellow
banana

yellow
jumper

yellow duck

yellow sponge

blue

Blue dress for a blue-sky day.
Why don't you come out and play?

Discuss with your child the different shades of blue she can see. Explain to her that we call all of these colours 'blue'.

Point to the blue things you can play with.

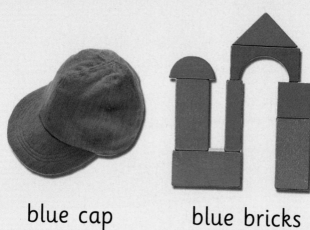

blue cap

blue bricks

blue paper and crayons

blue car

green

Green is bright, just like a tree.
I think green looks great on me.

When you are in the garden or park, look for
different shades of green. Use words like
'lighter', 'paler', 'darker', etc to describe them.

What green things can you see here?

green
T-shirt

green
painting

green
watering can

green
leaf

Can you tidy your own toys into groups and colours?

blue

red

Look at all the colours on the train!

yellow

green

What colour is the funnel?

What colour is the roof?

Mixing paints is so much fun.

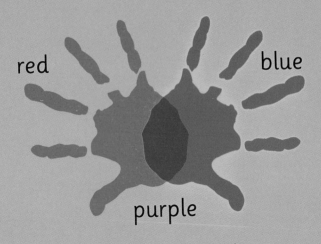

red   blue

purple

Red and blue make purple.

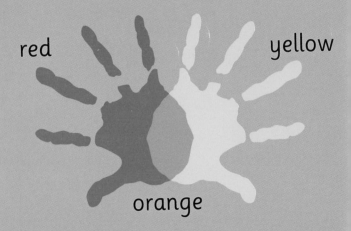

red   yellow

orange

Red and yellow make orange.